Disasters

on the MAP

Alix Wood

PowerKiDS press

New York

Published in 2015 by Rosen Publishing
29 East 21st Street, New York, NY 10010

Copyright © 2015 by the Rosen Publishing Group, Inc.
Produced for Rosen by Alix Wood Books

Editor for Alix Wood Books: Eloise Macgregor
Designer: Alix Wood
US Editor: Joshua Shadowens
Researcher: Kevin Wood
Geography Consultant: Kerry Shepheard, B.Ed (Hons) Geography

Photo Credits: Cover © imagist/Shutterstock; 4 © topora/Shutterstock;
26 © Rick Whitacre/Shutterstock; 5 bottom (a), 17 bottom © public domain;
18 bottom © Gobierno de Chile; 21 © NOAA; 28 © Alicia M. Garcia/DoD;
all other images © Shutterstock

Publisher's Cataloging Data

Wood, Alix.
Disasters on the map / by Alix Wood.
p. cm. — (Fun with map skills)
Includes index.
ISBN 978-1-4777-6976-8 (library binding) — ISBN 978-1-4777-6977-5 (pbk.) —
ISBN 978-1-4777-6978-2 (6-pack)
1. Disasters—Juvenile literature. 2. Navigation—History—Juvenile literature.
3. Maps —Juvenile literature. I. Wood, Alix. II. Title.
GB5019.W69 2015
910.4—d23

Manufactured in the United States of America

CPSIA Compliance Information: Batch #WS14PK9: For Further Information contact Rosen Publishing, New York, New York at 1-800-237-9932

Contents

Mapping Disasters

A disaster can be natural or man-made. A ship hitting a rock at sea might happen because the captain was not aware that the rock was there. Accurate maps and map reading skills can help people safely cross the oceans. A hurricane is a strong wind that can destroy everything in its path. Maps can help predict where natural events, such as hurricanes or earthquakes, may hit.

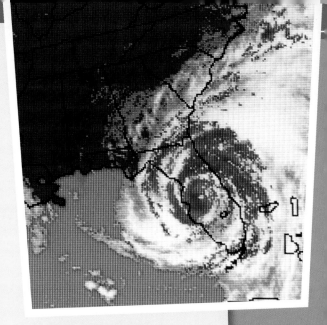

▲ A map showing a hurricane over Florida.

A map is a diagram of the Earth's surface, or of part of it. There are many types of map that could help during a disaster. Weather forecasters can create weather maps that show changes in temperature, wind speed, or rainfall. Maps of the ocean floor can help predict where earthquakes might happen. Sea charts can show a ship's captain where obstacles are at high and low tide to help prevent shipwrecks like the one below.

Do You Know?

Warning systems help people prepare for a disaster. Bangladesh has a cyclone early warning system which has saved many thousands of lives. The warning system gives people time to prepare before the strong winds arrive on land.

A map drawn on a globe is almost the same shape as the Earth itself. Because it is the same shape, a globe can show how the Earth really looks. It can't show you much close-up detail, though. Globe views of the Earth can help track the weather. Flat maps can be more useful than globes. They can fold up and go in your pocket or fit on your cellphone screen. Maps can show more detail than a globe because mapmakers can choose smaller areas to zoom in on.

▲ A globe can help follow the path of natural disasters.

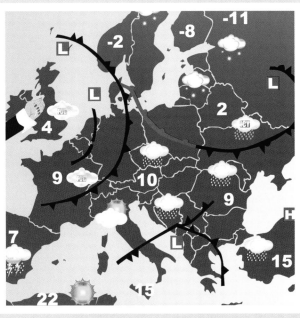

▲ A flat map can focus on a smaller area's weather.

Try Your Skills

Which type of map on the right would you use for each of these tasks below?

1. Check for hot weather that might cause a forest fire.

2. Guide a ship safely through some rocks.

3. Predict where earthquake damage may occur.

a) A sea chart

b) A weather forecast

c) A map showing an earthquake

Predicting Floods Using Maps

Meteorologists make weather maps using infomation from many different weather-recording instruments. A weather station usually records the temperature, how far you can see, the wind speed, rainfall, and the **atmospheric pressure**. They also use images taken by satellites, and information from weather balloons high in the sky to get their information. Meteorologists can then make maps showing what weather is to be expected in different areas of the world.

Weather maps can warn people of possible weather disasters such as flooding. Heavy rain can cause flooding when rivers or streams overflow their banks. Large storms or earthquakes under the sea can cause the sea to rise and rush inland, too.

Do You Know?

Floods are the second most common natural disaster on Earth, after wildfires.

Try Your Skills

Maps use symbols to show where features are. Symbols are clear, simple drawings. Can you match these weather map symbols with the types of weather below?

1.    2.   3.

a) sun
b) strong winds
c) rain

Meteorologists watch the skies looking for large clouds that could produce heavy rainfall. They also measure rainfall using special measuring instruments, like the one in the picture on the right. Meteorologists can work out the usual rainfall for an area. If the rain becomes heavier than normal, the ground may become unable to soak up any more water. Then flooding may occur.

► Rain gauges should be placed in the open, away from buildings or trees.

Types of Clouds

Even though all clouds contain water, only some types will cause rain. Meteorologists need to know the differences between the types of cloud so that they can predict what weather the clouds will bring. Low level clouds are the rain bearing clouds. Stratus clouds may bring drizzle. Nimbostratus clouds can bring heavy rain. The tall cumulonimbus clouds are also called thunderclouds. They can produce heavy rainstorms.

Take a look out of the window. See if you can guess what sort of clouds you can see in the sky.

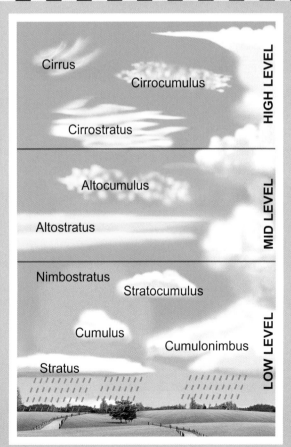

Earthquakes!

There are several million earthquakes around the world every year. Earthquakes cause the Earth to shake. They happen because the Earth is made up of around 20 different plates that move slowly in different directions. Sometimes the plates knock together, move apart, or slide against each other. These movements are what cause earthquakes.

Earthquakes are measured using the Richter Scale. Earthquakes registering below 4 are very small. The largest recorded earthquake was in Chile in 1960. It registered 9.5 on the Richter scale!

Scale	Description	Effect	Average per year
4	Minor	Noticeable shaking	6,200
5	Moderate	Can cause some damage	800
6	Strong	Destructive	120
7	Major	Serious damage	18
8 or more	Great	Serious damage over a large area	1

Do You Know?

The point on the Earth's surface directly above the source of the earthquake is called the **epicenter**.

Mapping Fault Lines On A Grid

Look at the map below. The red lines on the map show where the Earth's plates meet. These borders are where earthquakes may occur. They are called fault lines. Active volcanoes also occur along these plate boundaries. On top of the map there is a grid. A grid helps with map reading as it divides the map into squares. You can tell someone exactly what square a place is to help them find it. First find the number along the x **axis**. Then find the number that goes up the y axis. You can remember the order by saying "Go along the corridor and then up the stairs." You write a grid reference like this (2, 1). You always write the number that belongs to the bottom left hand corner of the square first.

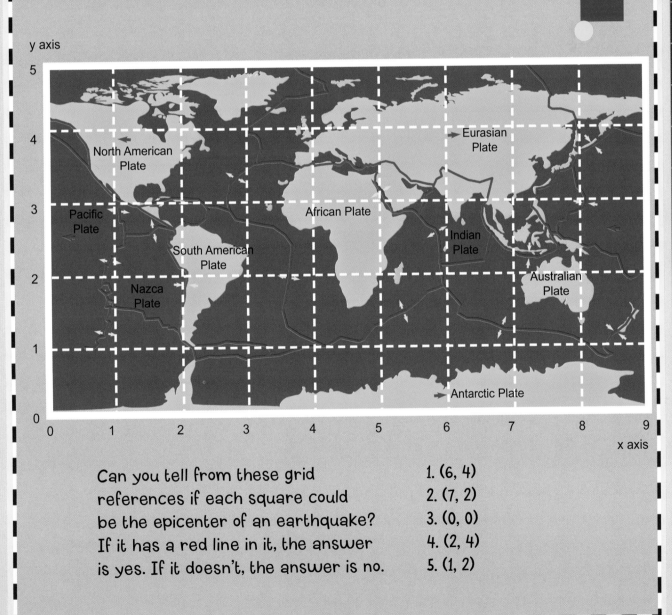

Can you tell from these grid references if each square could be the epicenter of an earthquake? If it has a red line in it, the answer is yes. If it doesn't, the answer is no.

1. (6, 4)
2. (7, 2)
3. (0, 0)
4. (2, 4)
5. (1, 2)

Volcanoes!

A volcano is a mountain with a **crater** in the center. Hot, **molten** rock from deep inside the Earth sometimes erupts through the crater. Gases and rock shoot up through the opening. Volcanoes tend to be centered around where plates join, just like earthquakes. Volcanoes can be either "extinct," "dormant," or "active." An extinct volcano will most likely never erupt again. A dormant volcano has not erupted in 2,000 or more years. Some dormant volcanoes recharge over hundreds of thousands of years. An active volcano has erupted recently and may erupt again.

One of the most volcanic regions of the world is called the Pacific Ring of Fire. It follows the coasts of the Pacific Ocean from New Zealand up through Indonesia and Japan on its west side and then back down the coasts of North and South America to its east. The volcanoes in Indonesia are among the most active of the Pacific Ring of Fire. In Java, the volcano Merapi has erupted more than 80 times since the year 1,000.

Pacific Ring of Fire

Do You Know?

Volcanoes can also be found on the ocean floor and even under icecaps! The word "volcano" comes from Vulcan, the Roman god of fire.

The islands of Java were mostly created by volcanic eruptions. Look at the map below and see if you can see the volcanoes along the mountain range. These small islands have around 45 active volcanoes on them! Imagine you want to go and see some of these volcanoes. Get some paper and write down the grid references you need to find the volcanoes below.

1. Merapi   2. Krakatau   3. Bromo   4. Slamet

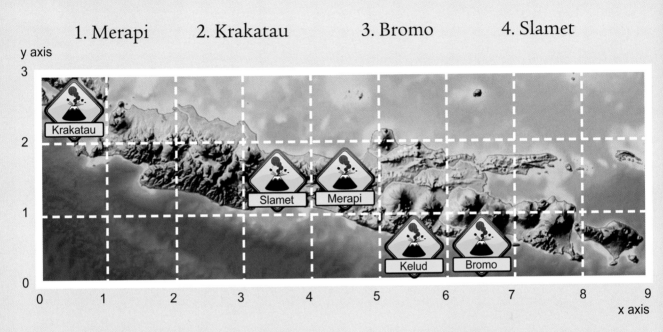

Move To Volcano Island

Your family is moving to Volcano Island. Look at the weather facts below and try and work out which house would be safest to live in.

- Volcanic ash clouds produce **acid rain**.

- The wind on Volcano Island always blows from west to east.

- Two of the Earth's plates meet under the bridge

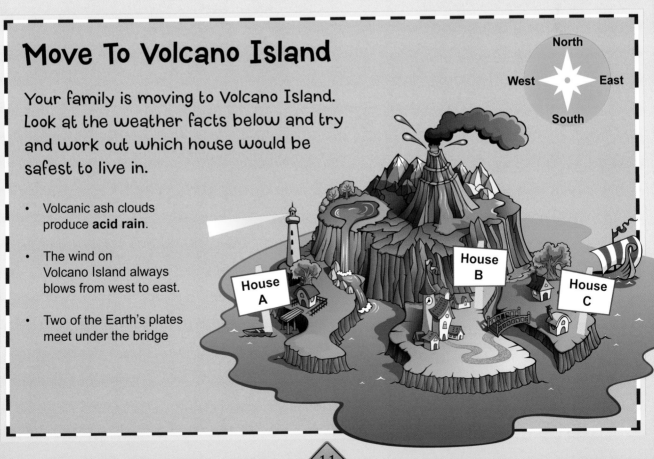

Dangerous Winds

Hurricanes are storms with violent winds. The hurricane clouds can be 600 miles (966 km) across! The winds can spiral at speeds up to 200 miles (322 km) per hour. They form over warm ocean water. The moist air rises and more moist air fills the space left below. This movement of air creates a circular motion creating a spiraling wind.

▲ hurricane damage

The Earth is divided by imaginary lines of **longitude** and **latitude** to help people locate places on a map. Latitude lines run across the Earth. Longitude lines go up and down. Hurricanes usually form between 5 to 15 degrees latitude north and south of the **equator**. The equator runs along the middle of the Earth, at 0 degrees latitude. Degrees are sometimes written like this "º."

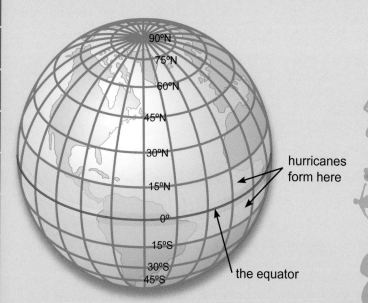

90ºN
75ºN
60ºN
45ºN
30ºN
15ºN
0º
15ºS
30ºS
45ºS

hurricanes form here

the equator

Do You Know?

A natural force makes fluids veer right when north of the equator and veer left when south of the equator. Because of this, hurricanes go **counterclockwise** if they are north of the equator, and **clockwise** if they are south of it!

▶ The center of the storm is called the "eye." It is the calmest part of the hurricane. Surrounding the eye is the "eye wall," where the storm's most violent winds are.

the eye

the eye wall

Typhoons, Cyclones, and Hurricanes

What's the difference? Hurricanes, typhoons, and cyclones are actually all the same thing. They are called different names just because of where they are! A cyclone is ANY rotating low pressure system. A hurricane is a cyclone that happens over the Atlantic or the eastern Pacific Ocean. A cyclone over the western Pacific Ocean is called a typhoon. A cyclone over the Indian Ocean is called a cyclone.

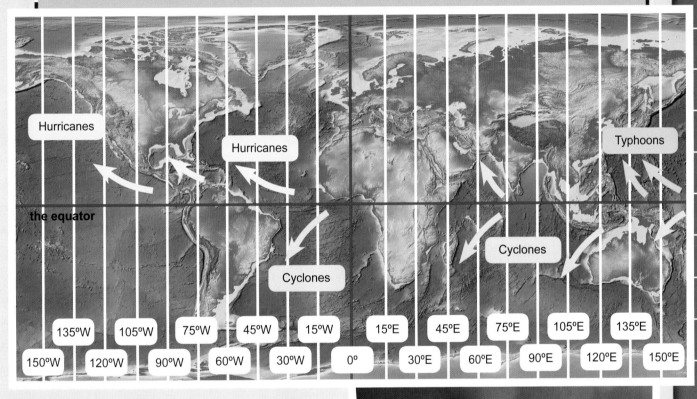

Hurricanes

Hurricanes

Typhoons

the equator

Cyclones

Cyclones

Cyclones

135ºW	105ºW	75ºW	45ºW	15ºW	15ºE	45ºE	75ºE	105ºE	135ºE

150ºW	120ºW	90ºW	60ºW	30ºW	0º	30ºE	60ºE	90ºE	120ºE	150ºE

Try Your Skills

The map above shows the lines of longitude that divide the Earth up from top to bottom. Can you say if the cyclones below are typhoons, hurricanes or cyclones from the locations below?

1. 105ºW
2. 15ºW south of the equator
3. 150ºE north of the equator
4. 60ºE

▲ A tornado is a funnel-shaped cyclone that can happen during thunderstorms. They can happen anywhere in the world.

13

Wind and Fire

Wildfires can destroy huge areas of land. They can be caused by lightning, volcanoes erupting, or by human carelessness. Sometimes people start fires on purpose. Heat waves, dry weather, and strong winds all help to start and spread deadly fires.

Firefighters know that fires need fuel, air, and heat to burn. Firefighters can take away the fuel that the fire needs by clearing the area of dry trees and grass, so that the fire has nothing to burn. They use a special tool that is a combination of an ax and a hoe. If the fire is too large, planes and helicopters will drop water and special chemicals that will smother and cool the flames. Teams may be given **compass directions** to locate the right place to tackle the blaze. Do you know your compass directions?

Try Your Skills

A compass has a magnetic needle which points north. Drawn on the compass is a **compass rose**. The compass rose shows the four main **cardinal directions**, north, south, east, and west.

Using the compass rose on the picture on the left, which direction from the center of the fire are these places on the map?

1. The firetruck?
2. The lake?
3. The forest?
4. The house?

Intermediate directions are halfway between the four cardinal directions of north, south, east, and west. The intermediate directions are northeast, northwest, southeast, and southwest. They are usually shortened to NE, NW, SE, and SW.

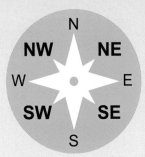

Wind Direction

Wind will spread a fire in the direction it is blowing. A change of wind direction can mean a change in tactics for the firefighters! There is a fire in the center of this map. Can you decide which building the fire may spread to in each of these wind conditions? Use the compass rose above to help you.

1. Northeasterly 2. Southwesterly 3. Westerly

Do You Know?

Winds are always known by the direction they are heading. A northeast wind comes from the southwest and heads northeast.

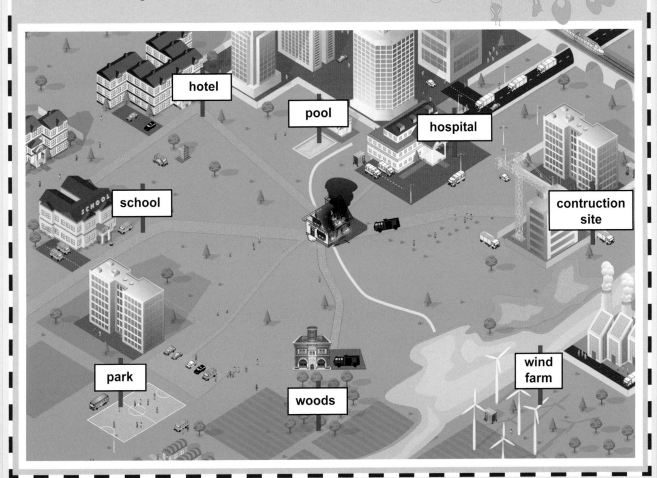

Avoiding Shipwrecks

Navigating a huge passenger ship through the oceans is not easy. Charts must show the depth of the sea and mark every rock and tiny island so that the captain can make sure the ship doesn't hit anything. Look at the key on this map. The key shows you what the symbols mean on a map. Can you tell which of the routes below would be the safest? You don't want to hit an obstacle or the shallows!

Journey A —— ——   Journey B ▬▬ ▬▬   Journey C ▭▭ ▭▭   Journey D ▬▬ ▬▬

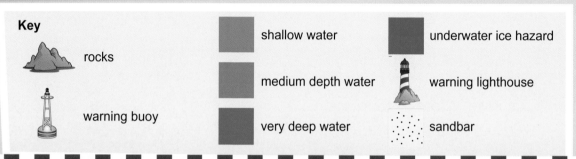

Key

rocks

warning buoy

shallow water

medium depth water

very deep water

underwater ice hazard

warning lighthouse

sandbar

Icebergs

Navigating a boat around icebergs is very difficult. An iceberg is a massive floating body of ice that has broken away from a glacier. Only about 10 percent of an iceberg is above the surface of the water. The rest is hidden below the surface of the sea. A ship can think it is sailing around an iceberg, but still hit it as the iceberg is larger below the water. People can't map icebergs, as they move through the ocean rather than stay in one place.

One of the most well-known shipping disasters was the sinking of the passenger liner the RMS *Titanic* in 1912. The *Titanic* sailed through drifting ice on her way from England to New York. South of Newfoundland she struck an iceberg and started to sink. The ship did not have enough lifeboats and the waters were freezing cold. Between 1,490 and 1,635 people died.

▲ The RMS *Titanic* preparing for her voyage from Southampton, England.

Do You Know?

After the *Titanic* disaster, the International Ice Patrol was formed. They report the location of icebergs in the North Atlantic using information from ships and aircraft in the area. There have been no fatal iceberg collision since the patrol was formed!

Mining Disasters

Maps of an area's geology help mining engineers know what **minerals** may be found in certain areas of rock. These maps also help engineers design the safest way to mine the minerals. Mining accidents can happen. Leaks of poisonous or explosive natural gases are dangerous. Underground explosions or machinery vibrations can cause mines to collapse. Flooding can be a big problem too.

▲ Engineers look at diagrams of mine layouts to help improve safety.

In August 2010, 33 miners trapped underground in Chile were glad the mines were well mapped. With the help of detailed maps rescuers worked out where the men might be and drilled **boreholes** close to a rescue shelter. Seventeen days after the collapse the rescuers pulled out one of the drills and found a note taped to the drill bit! The note said in big red letters "We are well in the shelter, the 33 of us." Knowing that they were alive, the rescuers started drilling a larger hole. After 69 days trapped underground, all the men were brought safely to the surface!

Do You Know?

While one of the miners was 2,300 feet (701 m) underground his wife gave birth to a daughter. He named her Esperanza, which is Spanish for "hope."

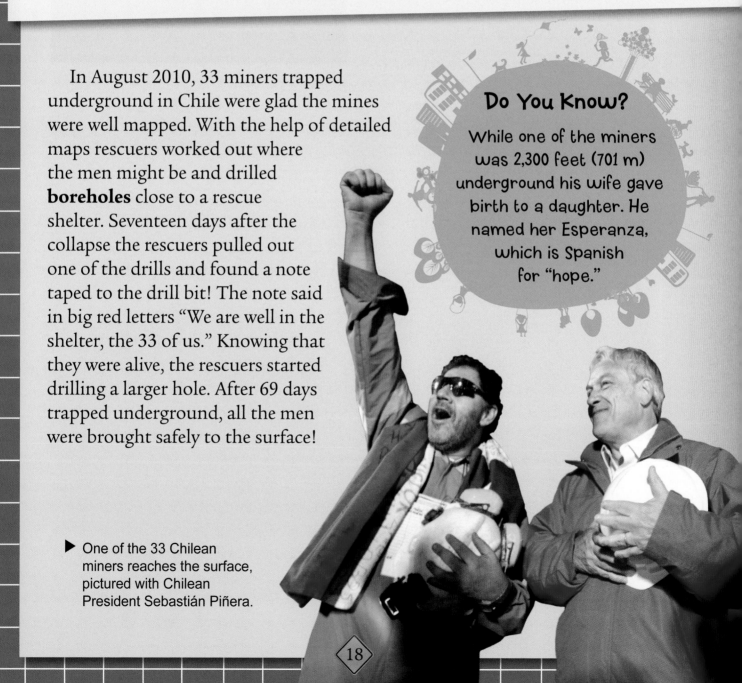

▶ One of the 33 Chilean miners reaches the surface, pictured with Chilean President Sebastián Piñera.

It's important to learn how to give and follow directions. You can use simple directions such as "turn left," or "go up." You can use landmarks to help direct people too, such as saying "go straight on past the store" or "turn left by the school." The problem with the word "left" is the direction changes if you turn around. It's better to use points of the compass to direct people, such as "go east on Baker Street."

Try Your Skills

Can you direct the rescuers to the trapped miner? Look at the instructions below. Which set of instructions will reach the trapped miner safely?

1. Go down shaft 2 to level 1. Head east. Pass shaft 3.

2. Go down shaft 1 to level 3. Head east to shaft 2. Go down to level 4. Head east to shaft 3. Go up to level 2 and head east.

3. Go down shaft 1 to level 3. Head east to shaft 2. Go down to level 4. Head east to shaft 3. Go up to level 3 and head east.

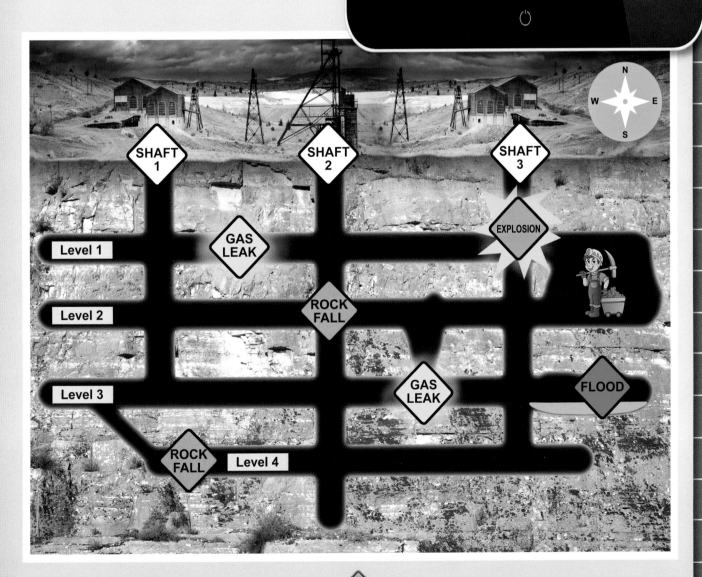

Tsunami Waves

Tsunamis are enormous waves caused by an earthquake, or by a volcano erupting underwater. The energy of the earthquake or volcano causes the water level to rise. The water spreads into a powerful wave that travels at incredible speed. The waves can be over 100 feet (30 m) high. They can cause severe damage if they strike land. A tsunami gets bigger as it gets closer to shore. When it hits shallow water the huge wave travels more slowly. The wave pulls back the water near the shore and increases in height before it hits land.

▲ The water on the coast recedes before a big tsunami wave hits.

Places where tsunamis are likely will usually have warning systems to alert people of the danger. Local people will learn nature's warning signs that a tsunami may be on the way, too.

1. An earthquake can be felt
2. The sea suddenly pulls back leaving bare sand
3. Animals start to behave oddly

Once you can see the wave, it is usually too late to get away. Head for high ground that is as far inland as possible.

Do You Know?

The Japanese word *tsunami* means "harbor wave."

20

Tsunami Time Map

This map below shows how much time it takes for a tsunami to reach different areas of the world. This kind of map can be very useful to warn people about a tsunami and give them enough time to get to safety. Each different colored band equals an hour in time. The star marks the epicenter of the earthquake.

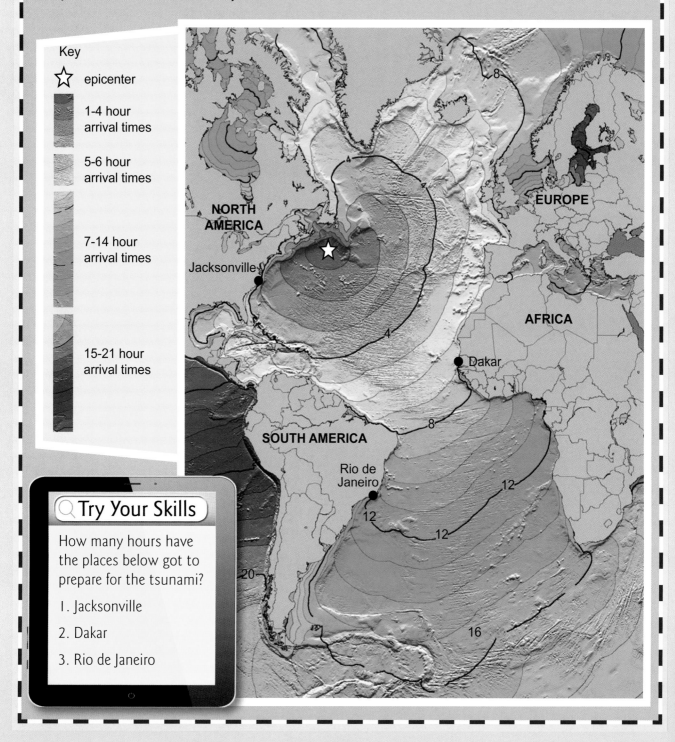

Key

☆ epicenter

1-4 hour arrival times

5-6 hour arrival times

7-14 hour arrival times

15-21 hour arrival times

🔍 Try Your Skills

How many hours have the places below got to prepare for the tsunami?

1. Jacksonville
2. Dakar
3. Rio de Janeiro

Hot, Dry Weather

All types of weather can be both good and bad. Heavy rain can cause dangerous flooding. But no rain can cause a drought. A drought is a period where there has not been enough rainfall, and rivers and streams dry up. Plants and animals can die. A drought increases the risk of fire. Flash floods are common too, as when it finally does rain the ground is too hard for the water to soak into.

Scientists study the world's weather looking for any changes. People are worried that pollution has made a hole in the **ozone layer** that protects the Earth from the Sun's strong rays. This means that the Earth may be gradually getting warmer. Scientists study temperatures and create maps showing the weather now, and what they think the weather will be like in the future. These maps help us see if we have a problem, and help us plan ahead.

Do You Know?

The water that we use today is the same water that existed a billion years ago! Water is recycled by nature. The Sun pulls water up into the clouds, and the clouds rain it back down again.

The **climate** is the weather conditions in a particular area. Australia is a large country with several different climates. It is in the southern hemisphere, south of the equator. The north of Australia is warm and has a tropical climate.

· The north has a rainy season from December to March.

· The middle of Australia is very hot in summer.

· The south of Australia is closer to Antarctica and has very cold winters.

Try Your Skills

You are planning a long trip across Australia visiting Darwin, Tennant Creek, Alice Springs, Adelaide, and Canberra. Which of the trips below is the best to avoid the hot weather and the bad rains? Use the map and other information to help you.

Trip 1. February - Canberra
March - Adelaide
April - Alice Springs
May - Tennant Creek
June - Darwin

Trip 2. December - Darwin
January - Tennant Creek
February - Alice Springs
March - Adelaide
April - Canberra

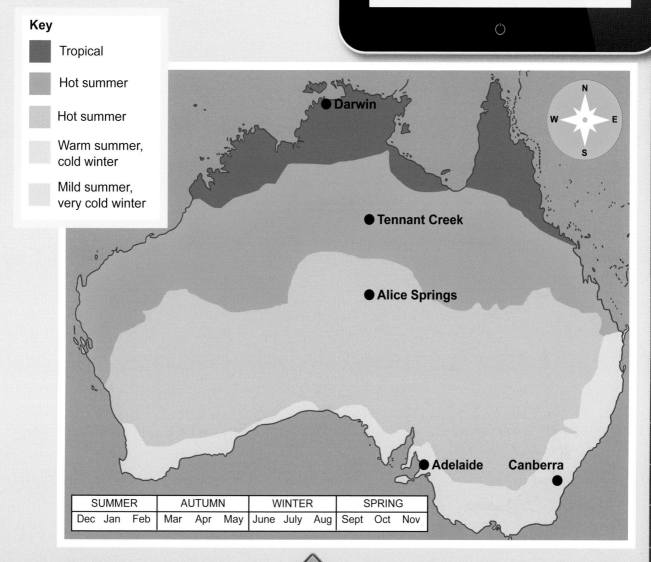

Key

Tropical

Hot summer

Hot summer

Warm summer, cold winter

Mild summer, very cold winter

● Darwin

● Tennant Creek

● Alice Springs

● Adelaide   Canberra ●

SUMMER			AUTUMN			WINTER			SPRING		
Dec	Jan	Feb	Mar	Apr	May	June	July	Aug	Sept	Oct	Nov

Predicting Disasters

Weather maps often have lines drawn on them. What do the lines mean? The lines will probably either be isotherms, isobars, or isotachs. *Iso* is the Greek word for "equal." An isotherm is a line on a map connecting points which have the same temperature. An isobar connects points that have the same pressure. An isotach connects points where the wind speeds are the same.

▲ This map shows isobars and weather fronts.

Weather fronts show a change in air temperature. A cold front is colored blue. It is where warm and cold air meet and the cold replaces the warm. A warm front is colored red. It is where cold and warm air meet, too, but warm air replaces the cold. An occluded front is colored purple. It is where a cold front and a warm front join. The direction of the circles or triangles shows the direction the front is moving.

cold front   warm front   occluded front

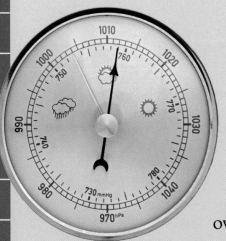

▲ a barometer

Changes in temperature, pressure, and wind strength and direction all help predict what weather a region can expect in the next few days. Many people have barometers in their homes. When you tap the glass the needle swings around. The needle shows if the pressure is rising or falling. A slowly rising pressure over a week or two usually means we can expect the weather to stay like it is. A sudden drop in pressure over a few hours may mean a storm is coming.

Which Map Is Best?

Can you decide which type of map you need to find the answer to each of these questions? Look at the information below and on page 24 to help you.

1. Check for dangerous winds

2. Try to predict if the air pressure will mean a change in the weather

3. Monitor the ocean temperature

a)

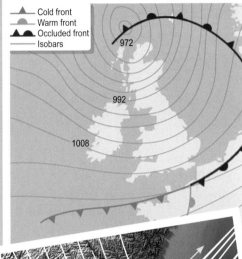

b)

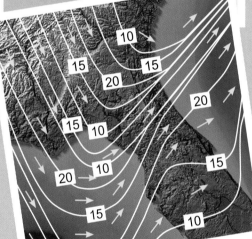

c)

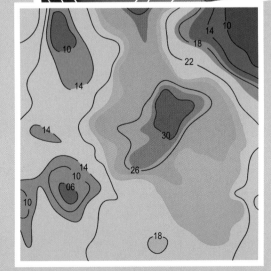

Map a)
This map shows the isobars over the United Kingdom. Isobars measure the difference in air pressure.

Map b)
This map shows the isotachs over Florida. Isotachs measure wind speed. The map also shows the wind direction.

Map c)
This map shows the isotherms over an island in the ocean. Isotherms measure temperature. On this map some of the lines are colored in to help show the differences in temperature. The blue areas are colder than the red areas.

Avalanche!

Snow can be dangerous. An avalanche is a mass of snow or ice that suddenly crashes down a moutainside. It can cause damage to property and people can get trapped beneath the snow. Most avalanches are triggered by people skiing, snowboarding, walking, or snowmobiling on the snow. Other causes of avalanches are a very heavy snowfall, steep bare slopes, vibrations from an earthquake, and melting snow that freezes creating a slippery surface for new snowfall.

In the Alps, a mountain range in Europe, most avalanches occur between January and March. To try to predict if an avalanche is likely, experts study weather information. The snow on the mountainside is collected to try to forecast whether an avalanche may happen. Sometimes avalanches are started deliberately using explosives, in order to prevent the snow building up.

Do You Know?

A large avalanche can reach speeds of 80 miles (130 km) per hour, in about 5 seconds. Cracking sounds can warn you that an avalanche may be about to happen.

Degree of Avalanche danger

1	gering / faible / debole / low
2	mässig / limité / moderato / moderate
3	erheblich / marqué / marcato / considerable
4	gross / fort / forte / high
5	sehr gross / très fort / molto forte / very high

▲ An avalanche warning sign at a ski resort in the Alps.

A map's scale shows you how large the area is that the map covers. The scale lets you work out you how far one place is from another, too. Most maps will have the scale written on them. The scale uses one unit of measurement, for example an inch (cm) to represent another unit of measurement, such as a mile (km). This scale shows 1 inch = 1 mile, 1.58 cm = 1 km.

0   1   2   3 miles

0   1   2   3   4   5 km

Try Your Skills

To answer the questions in the map below, use a piece of string or cotton. Measure the string from the middle of the snowboarder to the middle of the risk in the picture of the ski resort. With a pen, mark the string at both points. Measure the marked string along the scale to find the distance between you and the avalanche risks.

How Close is Danger?

You are at a ski resort. Can you measure how many miles (km) away all the avalanche risks are from your picture on the ski resort picture? Use the scale and the information in the box above to help you.

a) skier   b) heavy snow   c) helicopter vibrations

measure using string like this

Monitoring the Weather

Satellites in the sky send images back to Earth that are very useful to mapmakers and weather watchers. Meteorologists can watch and track extreme weather as it travels around the globe. Dust storms happen when a strong wind blows loose dirt and sand from the dry land. They usually happen in times of very dry weather. Dust storms are dangerous on roads as the dust can make it impossible to see. The dust also helps spread diseases.

▶ A satellite image of a swirling dust storm.

In the photo below a massive dust storm cloud heads toward a military camp in Iraq. People who live near deserts that have dust storms rely on weather reports to warn them if one may happen. Severe storms can damage cars, property, and even lead to loss of life.

Do You Know?

Dust storms don't just happen on Earth! On Mars, large dust storms reach speeds of over 100 miles (160 km) per hour!

Make Your Own Wind Vane

You will need a drinking straw, a pair of scissors, a piece of thin cardstock, a piece of thick cardboard, a pin, a pencil with an eraser, a yogurt cup, some sticky tape, and a marker pen.

1. Ask an adult to cut a slot in both ends of the drinking straw.

2. Cut out two triangles from the thin cardstock. Push them into the slots in the drinking straw.

3. Stick a pin through the straw about half-way along its length. Then push the pin into the pencil eraser. Make sure that the straw can spin around.

4. Push the pencil through the top of a yogurt cup. You may need to make a small hole first with the scissors. Ask an adult to help you. Tape the container onto a piece of thick cardboard.

5. Mark N, E, S, and W on the card. Take the wind vane outside and see which way the wind is blowing!

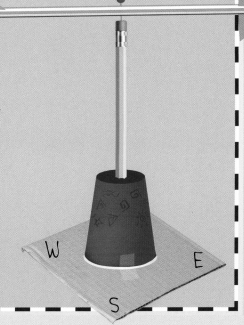

Glossary

acid rain (A-sud RAYN)
Rainfall made dangerously acidic by pollution of the atmosphere.

atmospheric pressure
(at-muh-SFEER-ik PREH-shur)
The pressure exerted by the weight of the atmosphere.

axis (AK-sus)
A number line (as an x-axis or a y-axis) along which coordinates are measured.

boreholes (BOHR-hohlz)
Holes that are drilled into the earth.

cardinal directions
(KAHRD-nul dih-REK-shunz)
The four principal points of the compass: north, south, east, west.

climate (KLY-mut)
The average weather conditions of a particular place or region over a period of years.

clockwise (KLOK-wyz)
In the direction in which the hands of a clock turn.

compass directions
(KUM-pus duh-REK-shunz)
The line or course along which something moves.

compass rose (KUM-pus ROHZ)
A drawing on a map which shows directions.

counterclockwise
(kown-ter-KLOK-wyz)
In the opposite direction in which the hands of a clock turn.

crater (KRAY-tur)
A hollow shaped like a bowl around the opening of a volcano.

epicenter (EH-pih-sen-ter)
The part of the Earth's surface directly above the starting point of an earthquake.

equator (ih-KWAY-tur)
An imaginary circle around the Earth everywhere equally distant from the north pole and the south pole.

intermediate direction
(in-ter-MEE-dee-et dih-REK-shun)
Northeast, northwest, southeast, or southwest.

latitude (LA-tih-tood)
Distance north or south from the equator measured in degrees.

longitude (LON-jih-tood)
Distance measured by degrees or time east or west from the prime meridian.

meteorologists
(mee-tee-uh-RAH-luh-jists)
Scientists that study the
atmosphere, weather, and
weather forecasting.

minerals (MIN-rulz)
Naturally occurring substances
such as ore, petroleum, or
water obtained usually from
the ground.

molten (MOHL-ten)
Melted especially by very
great heat.

navigating (NA-vuh-gayt-ing)
To direct one's course in a ship
or aircraft.

ozone layer (OH-zohn LAY-er)
A layer in the stratosphere that
contains ozone sufficient to
block most ultraviolet radiation
from the Sun.

satellites (SA-tih-lyts)
A man-made object or vehicle
intended to orbit the Earth, the
Moon, or another heavenly body.

Read More

Bakowski, Barbara. *Mapping Oceans*. New York: Cavendish Square,
   2011.

Close, Edward. *All About the Weather*. New York: PowerKids Press, 2014.

Portman, Michael. *Savage Tsunamis*. New York: Gareth Stevens, 2012.

Due to the changing nature of Internet links, PowerKids Press
has developed an online list of websites related to the subject
of this book. This site is updated regularly. Please use this link to
access the list:

www.powerkidslinks.com/fwms/disa/

Index

Answers

page 5
1. b, 2. a, 3. c
page 6
1. c, 2. a, 3. b
page 9
1. no, 2. yes, 3. no, 4. no, 5. yes
page 11
House A is safest to live in.
page 13
1. hurricane, 2. cyclone, 3. typhoon, 4. cyclone

page 14
1. east, 2. north, 3. west, 4. south
page 15
1. hospital, 2. park, 3. school
page 16
Journey A
page 19
no. 2 will reach the miners
page 21
1. 4 hours, 2. 7 hours, 3. 12 hours

page 23
trip 1
page 25
1. b, 2. a, 3. c
page 27
a) 2 miles (3.2 km)
b) 1 mile (1.6 km)
c) 3 miles (4.8 km)
page 29
1. c, 2. Majorca